Trainer's Manual

The Law Firm Associate's Guide to

Connecting with Your Colleagues

Barbara Miller ■ Martin Camp

ABA LawPracticeManagementSection

MARKETING • MANAGEMENT • TECHNOLOGY • FINANCE

Commitment to Quality: The Law Practice Management Section is committed to quality in our publications. Our authors are experienced practitioners in their fields. Prior to publication, the contents of all our books are rigorously reviewed by experts to ensure the highest quality product and presentation. Because we are committed to serving our readers' needs, we welcome your feedback on how we can improve future editions of this book.

Cover design by Andrew Alcala, ABA Publishing.

Library of Congress Cataloging-in-Publication Data
The Law Firm Associate's Guide to Connecting with Your Colleagues: Trainer's Manual. Barbara B. Miller and Martin L. Camp: Library of Congress Cataloging-in-Publication Data is on file.

10-digit: ISBN 1-60442-488-5
13-digit: ISBN 978-1-60442-488-1

11 10 09   5 4 3 2 1

Discounts are available for books ordered in bulk. Special consideration is given to state bars, CLE programs, and other bar-related organizations. Inquire at Book Publishing, American Bar Association, 321 N. Clark Street, Chicago, Illinois 60654.

CONTENTS

ABOUT THE AUTHORS

In very different roles, Barbara Miller and Martin Camp have taught, coached, inspired and motivated associate lawyers throughout the US, Asia, the Middle East, Europe and the UK.

As an independent consultant working in law firms since 1990, Barbara has helped associate lawyers adjust to law firm life and position their abilities to the highest and best use of the firm's clients. She has built a successful consulting business working with firms and their lawyers around the globe teaching effective communication and presentation skills toward the goal of successful firm advancement and client development. In the course of writing this book, she interviewed associates from around this country and saw that the pattern of problems and challenges repeated from firm to firm. She has worked with the National Association of Trial Advocacy and the National Practice Institute as a trainer and consultant.

As a 20-year partner and head of new associate development in the Dallas office of Jones Day for many years, Martin mentored and coached associate lawyers for effectiveness with both work products and professional relationships. In his current role as Assistant Dean for Student Affairs at the SMU Dedman School of Law, Martin teaches, inspires, and motivates future lawyers in their chosen career paths. Their combined perspectives and experiences provide a unique message for associate success in any law firm.

The authors have worked with thousands of lawyers and law students. They have seen the failures, but more importantly, they have witnessed the successes—those lawyers who have made the transition from student to "go to" associate. The authors believe you can develop the mentors, allies, and supporters who will help you along the way. And you can avoid creating enemies who can sabotage your progress.

INTRODUCTION: USING THE MANUAL

The exercises in this manual are meant to be starting points to allow lawyers in the firm to have the opportunity to interact with each other and to practice developing the skills addressed in *The Law Firm Associate's Guide to Connecting with Your Colleagues.*

There are many other ways to use the main text. Chapters could be assigned and read by associates to be discussed at periodic meetings, or trainers who are employed by the firm to work with associates in areas of communication or business development could be asked to facilitate workshops using the book and manual. Finally, the firm could develop additional case studies uniquely applicable to the firm culture and challenges. What is important is a commitment to addressing the issues associates face every day and the willingness to provide the resources they need to achieve success.

We have developed five scenarios that occur with some variation in law firms across the country; together they create a focus for applying the concepts presented in the main book. The exercises will illuminate approaches to each situation understanding that good communication is as much art as it is science; often there is no "right response." There are, however, attitudes and behaviors that will encourage maintaining relationships in the face of disagreement, managing emotion in the face of disapproval, and inspiring confidence and problem solving in the face of self-doubt and confusion. Our goal is to support, encourage, and train associate lawyers by applying effective communication skills and strategies that encourage productive and lasting professional relationships with their internal clients. Individual lawyers committed to their professional growth and professional development staff responsible for training lawyers can benefit from these ideas.

Throughout the manual you will find a number of quizzes or surveys for the participants to complete as well as some exercises. Some participants may be familiar with all or some of these tools. For others, it's their first exposure. Lawyers from diverse backgrounds may have varying initial responses to being asked to participate in this active aspect of the training. Care should be taken to explain in advance of the training that it is interactive so to provide the participants with both knowledge and practical skills. These tools have been effectively used in countless training sessions in many fields and are based upon solid research in the behavioral sciences. The level of success achieved in the training program will be impacted by the attitudes exemplified by the participants. While everyone should view this as an enjoyable experience, it is also a very serious one. The fact that the firm is investing the facilitator and participants' time and energy in the program is evidence of this fact and should be stressed. If you have a potentially large pool of participants, you may want to allow people to self-select into the first training session so that you insure a high level of buy-in and enthusiasm. Later some alumni can be enlisted to help explain the program and how they benefited to other potential participants.

You may also want to develop an evaluation tool to obtain feedback from the participants. Ask them which elements were the most and least beneficial and why. Request suggestions that they think will improve the program.

CHAPTER 1

Predictors of Success: Emotional Intelligence

As you begin to deconstruct the vignettes that follow, the Emotional Intelligence Quick Quiz and the preferred response sheet that accompanies it will begin to ground you in EQ concepts. Sometimes the preferred response is obvious. Sometimes a response is a combination of two approaches. As we say in the book, high IQs and stellar academic credentials are not the best predictors of success in life or law firms. One's emotional quotient, or EQ, includes the ability to respond professionally and appropriately to diverse people in diverse contexts. The creation and maintenance of powerful personal relationships using interpersonal skills produces trust and collaboration as you work on client teams. The human dimension of practicing law is rarely separated from excellent, even brilliant, legal analysis. In each of the following scenarios, a good EQ approach will strengthen the communication and therefore the outcome.

Emotional Intelligence Quick Quiz

Used with permission by Nicole Trimble, based on the book *Emotional Intelligence* by Daniel Goleman; Bantam Dell, 1995.

1. You've entered a conference room with other lawyers, associates and partners, who are about to begin a practice group meeting regarding the status and staffing needs of various cases. An argument breaks out between two senior attorneys. What do you do?
   a. Check your Blackberry for e-mails or appointments, paying little attention to the conversation.
   b. Become vigilantly observant of the conversation in an effort to understand what's happening and to see if and how it will be resolved.
   c. A little of both a and b.
   d. Not sure—didn't realize anything unusual was happening.

2. You've taken a group of kids to play soccer in the neighborhood park and one of them gets angry and upset because the others won't let them play. What do you do?
   a. Stay out of it—let the kids deal with it on their own.
   b. Talk with the child and help him/her figure out ways to get the other kids to play with them.
   c. Tell them nicely not to be upset.
   d. Try to distract the upset/angry child by suggesting other things to do.

3. In law school, you discovered you got a B in a course when you fully expected to receive an A. What do you do?
   a. Create a new strategy for graduating top in the class and resolve to follow through.
   b. Resolve to make all A's the remainder of law school.
   c. Tell yourself it really doesn't matter how well you do in the course and concentrate on the other courses.
   d. Go see the professor and try to talk her out of the grade.

4. You've volunteered to raise money for your law school and are in competition with others in your class to raise the most. Ten people in a row have turned you down. What do you do?
   a. Call it a day and hope you have better luck tomorrow.
   b. Assess your approach.
   c. Try something new in the next call and keep plugging away.
   d. Drop out of the competition.

5. You're chairing the diversity effort at your firm and you overhear someone telling a racist joke. What do you do?
   a. Ignore it—it's just a joke.
   b. Call or e-mail them with a reprimand.
   c. Speak up on the spot, saying that such jokes are inappropriate.
   d. Suggest they go through a diversity training program.

6. A close female friend, another associate, is furious with a male opposing counsel for ending a phone conversation with, "Hey, I've just read an article that says men are smarter than women. Want me to send it to you?" What do you say to her?
   a. Tell her to forget it—the guy's a jerk and the case is over and she doesn't have to deal with him again.

  b. Tell her you'll take her to lunch to forget about it.

  c. Tell her to get over it.

  d. Tell her about a similar situation in your past and you felt the same but then you heard his firm disciplined or fired him.

7. You and another associate and good friend are working closely on a project and now you've gotten into an argument that escalated into a shouting match. In the heat of the argument, you each make personal accusations you don't mean. What's the best thing to do?

  a. Take a 20-minute break and then continue the discussion.

  b. Just stop the argument—go silent, no matter what your friend says.

  c. Say you're sorry and ask for their apology too.

  d. Stop for a moment, collect your thoughts, and then state your side of the argument as precisely as you can.

8. You've been assigned to head a committee to look into associate retention in your firm. What's the first thing you do?

  a. Draw up an agenda and time slots for each of the issues so the committee can make efficient use of their time.

  b. Gather the committee for a get-to-know-you lunch.

  c. Begin by asking each person for ideas for solving the problem.

  d. Start with a brainstorming session, encouraging even the wildest ideas.

9. A highly prized first-year associate is aware he/she has a real shyness issue and never speaks up at section meetings or attends firm receptions or non-mandatory lunches. You persuaded him/her to choose your firm and you know, long-term, he/she must become more socialized and comfortable out from behind the desk. What do you do?

  a. Accept him/her as he/she is.

  b. Suggest a psychologist you know who would be able to help.

  c. Make an effort to bring him/her with you to your firm events and after work gatherings to help with the socialization process.

  d. With his/her permission create an ongoing series of manageable settings where he/she can practice small talk.

10. You resolved at the beginning of the year to take up tennis and now you've started. How do you approach your inner athleticism?
    a. Hold yourself to a strict practice time each day.
    b. Play with good players so you'll be stretched.
    c. Play only when you feel like it.
    d. Take lots of lessons, but struggle to find practice time.

Emotional Intelligence Quick Quiz
Key to Responses

There may be some value to any of the responses, but the preferred response suggests the best use of emotional intelligence concepts that are designed for participation in long-term relationships and adult attitudes.

1. Anything but d.

   Going unconscious or into denial is the last behavior choice if you are to demonstrate your ability to navigate dynamic professional relationships when the stakes are high and emotions are strong.

2. b.

   The a. response is passive and allows no opportunity to learn from the experience.

   The c. response doesn't validate feelings, no matter how reactionary they may be.

   The d. response will only relieve tension temporarily.

3. a.

   The b. response, without a strategy, has no meat to it.

   The c. response puts you into denial and you may lose the emotional energy to resolve.

   The d. response suggests the professor gave you a grade you didn't earn yourself. Is it really someone else's fault?

4. b.

   The a. response presumes success is just luck.

   The c. response is close but without assessing and/or analyzing what you are doing, you're just taking a stab in the dark.

   d. Assessment can be learned with commitment and persistence.

5. c.
   a. You would be out of integrity.
   b. Delaying your response suggests no deep alignment or commitment to the cause.
   The d. response still keeps *you* at a distance from the issue.

6. d. This creates empathy and rapport.
   a., b., and c. responses ignore real feelings and encourage denial. Answer a. could be modified to create more empathy ("I have had to deal with jerks like that before") and to acknowledge that the feelings of anger and frustration are valid ("I remember how angry I felt") and brought to closure ("At least you don't have to deal with that jerk all the time. I am so glad we don't work for him.").

7. a.
   The b. response is a control strategy and doesn't communicate collaboration.
   The c. response is also a control strategy.
   The d. response is close to good but taking a 20-minute break is better.

8. d. both inclusive and focused
   The a. response presumes that control and efficiency are the highest priorities of the committee's activity.
   The b. response lacks focus on the task.
   The c. response moves too quickly to solutions and may inhibit a creative process that will create solutions.

9. d.
   The a. response insures a short career at the firm and denies your role in the associate being at the firm at all.
   The b. response relieves you of any responsibility.
   The c. response is close but the creation of small steps first is preferable.

10. b.
    The a. response ignores the reality of contemporary law firm schedules. Because it's unrealistic, it sets you up to fail.
    The c. response ignores "resolve" in the scenario.
    The d. response sets you up for failure.

REVIEW AND DEBRIEFING

Look at your responses in light of the Answer Key to Responses and try to determine a pattern or patterns in the responses. All participants, but particularly those with low scores, should be encouraged to assess their strengths and weaknesses and determine what they can do in the future to insure a more effective emotional response to similar scenarios. Periodically reviewing this test can be a helpful reminder of the options you have when facing stressful situations in your career.

CHAPTER 2

Predictors of Success:
Setting and Achieving Goals

Countless studies have been conducted and books written about the importance of planning, prioritizing, and goal setting in achieving success. These techniques can be applied to all areas of your life. In the main book, Chapter 4, "Predictors of Success," explains that the predictors are attitudes and not IQ's. There are several types of intelligences, each with their separate matrices. Chapter 9, "Owning Your Career," of the main book discusses taking responsibility for the creation of your chosen vocation. All the chapters repeat the need to plan and implement.

The purpose of this section of the manual is to encourage all participants to set and achieve realistic short-, medium-, and long-term goals in the important areas of their lives. It is to both cope with the reality of daily demands and to challenge participants to consider the possibilities for their lives.

All participants should be encouraged to share their goals with someone whom they trust and who will encourage and support them to persevere. Spouses and significant others as well as mentors and supervisors should understand how to be supportive. Friends can be a great help in keeping you on track when they are aware of what you're trying to do.

Goals can be divided into duration (short-, medium-, and long-term) and by area of your life (career, relationship, personal health/spirit). Participants should set aside a block of uninterrupted time, alone. They should be encouraged to write the answers to questions like the following, as a primer for goal setting and to assess where they are in their current life path.

1) What do I see myself doing in five years? In ten?
2) What is the one thing I am most proud of in my life?

3) What one thing would I change if I could relive my life?
4) If there were no restrictions in my life, what would I be doing today?
5) What things give me the most joy?
6) I hate doing _____
7) I need to change the following behaviors because I feel out of control in these areas of my life _____

These are just a few of the types of questions that people can ask themselves to get an assessment of where they are and a glimpse of what they would like to do. It is important to establish this baseline in order to begin goal planning.

After taking this time for self-evaluation, the participant should be encouraged to write out short-term, medium-term and long-term goals in the three areas we have identified: career, relationship, and health/spirit. These goals are to be followed by written action steps—concrete changes that can be taken to achieve them.

Goal achievement includes daily planning. Taking just five minutes each day to plan makes a major difference in productivity. Too many confuse the urgent with the important and spend their days being buffeted by the winds of crisis instead of getting the most important things done. Chapter 10, "Managing Conflicting Expectations," in the main book is a good place to start in reviewing the importance of prioritization and managing expectations. Participants should commit to daily planning for one month. They will be amazed at the difference this one change will make. Daily planning involves not just a to-do list, but a true prioritization . . . "If I could only do one thing today, what would it be? What is the one thing I have to get done? What are the consequences of postponing this obligation? Is there anyone I can delegate all or part of this project to? Do I need to notify the assigning partner that I may not be able to complete this project on time?"

The chart on the next page addresses what the high achievers do so differently from the rest of the pack. Participants might use this chart as they set, review, revise, and achieve their goals. By writing down the goals, following through with daily action plans, then reviewing the goals and setting up benchmarks of success, participants will feel much more in control of their professional lives . . . because they will be!

CREATING AN ACTION PLAN

As outlined in Chapter 4, "Predictors of Success," of the main book character traits and strategic, assertive behavior are necessary when creating your career. Achievers take responsibility for their career success by developing relationships and creating positive visibility for themselves and their work; vigilance on these activities makes a real difference. Use the chart below for your action plan.

	Develop Alliances	Position Practice	Manage Perception
Daily	1. Courtesy to staff 2. Conversation with secretary 3. Questions to senior attorneys 4. 5.	1. Attend all section meetings 2. Listen for opportunities to add value 3. 4. 5.	1. Consider appropriate attire for the day's activity 2. Adjust behavior based on negative feedback 3. Be timely, prepared, focused, and rested 4. 5.
Weekly	1. Lunch with peers 2. Lunch with client 3. Review your firm's lawyer bios on the web 4. Attend Bar activities 5.	1. Check in with senior lawyers and/or clients 2. Review and update website bio regarding client work 3. Volunteer to lead a firm activity 4.	1. Seek feedback from peers re: meeting decorum 2. Review previous week's feedback and adjust 3. 4.
Monthly	1. E-mail legal colleagues for what's new 2. Civic board meeting 3. Meet with mentor 4. 5.	1. Attend client conferences, other legal issue seminars 2. E-mail clients with updates in industry 3. Write article or blog 4. Speak at public firm function 5.	1. Seek feedback specific to work product 2. Update personal part of website bio 3. 4.

CHAPTER 3

Scenario # 1:
Practice Group Switch

Many of the issues addressed in this scenario are discussed in Chapters 2, 4, 6, and 7 of the main book.

Monte is a third-year associate. He loves his firm and idolizes Mark, the partner for whom he works. Nevertheless, Monte has finally decided that Products Liabilities is not the area in which he wants to establish himself long-term. After three years of practice he has decided that labor and employment law is for him. The only problem is that Mark—the man who has taught him everything he knows about how to practice law, and Adam, the head of the Labor and Employment Section, do not even speak. Monte does not know why, but the men despise each other. Monte is afraid that telling Mark that he wants to switch practice groups (and in fact already had gotten clearance from the head of the Products Liability Section) will be viewed by Mark as a total betrayal. What's more, this will be especially awkward since they work in such a small office. But for the sake of his career, Monte believes that he has no choice. He walks into Mark's office, asks if he has a minute to talk, closes the door, and sits down.

Group Discussion Questions

1) What does Monte have to lose and what does he have to gain from having the conversation with Mark?
2) Would you have closed the door? Why or why not?
3) How would you begin the conversation?
4) Would you have gotten Adam's advice first about how to tell Mark?

In the main book, Chapter 2, "What Lawyers Need" deals with meeting people's needs. The most fundamental need is to feel comfortable. Explore the following:

5) How can Monte create comfort in Mark without fawning or patronizing him? *(Clue: Express gratitude and admiration.)*

6) How can Monte be relaxed to begin with? *(Clue: rehearse, exhale, speak his truth, and be quick—no over rationalizing.)*

7) What can Monte say to acknowledge Mark's mentoring and expertise as special and different from other lawyers he's worked around? *(Clue: Autonomy and independence are needs of great importance to lawyers.)*

It would be natural for Mark to be cynical, or even just concerned, about Monte's decision. Explore the following:

8) What might Mark's oppositional questions of Monte be? What would Mark want Monte to be aware of and cautious about?

9) How can Monte acknowledge Mark's contribution to him personally and professionally, again without fawning or patronizing?

The following are some exercises that can be used to prepare to deal with difficult conversations and situations. Relaxing the mind and body can become habits and used to help you remain calm and in control in the most stressful situations. The exercises can also help you avoid overreacting or giving inappropriate responses that can have damaging results to your effectiveness and others' perception of you. These same methods are used by successful athletes, business executives, actors, and others who have to achieve peak performance under difficult and stressful situations.

Exercises

A. Relaxation: Breathing

In advance of any anxiety-producing conversation, many will take a deep breath but then talk on a long, slow exhale. They need to inhale AND exhale, using their diaphragmatic muscle in addition to their lungs. This allows the speaker to start calmly and maintain clear thinking.

Have the group stand with their feet shoulder width apart, place their right hand on their abdominal muscle, which is attached to the diaphragm muscle about three inches below the belly button. Have them expel air as if they had been socked in the stomach and count to three. With their hand still on their belly, without heaving the shoulders have them push their hand out—get fat! Air will rush automatically to fill the vacuum and a relaxed feeling will follow. If extreme anxiety precedes a tough conversation, exhale, exhale, exhale, until calm overtakes the tension.

B. **Relaxation: Think Positively**

The purpose of this exercise is to create and maintain confidence in the face of discomfort and to eliminate terrorizing thoughts that can turn into a frenzy of anxiety. In the main book in Chapter 8, "The Importance of Feedback" we deal with the high achiever's inclination to be overly self-critical.

Monte might be thinking, "Mark will never be OK with this, but I've got to do it anyway. Now I feel like a schmuck; he has really been a good mentor and now I'm leaving. This won't go well, I just know it. I really want this conversation behind me. I sure hope he doesn't try and sabotage my switch—what if he does that? Then I'll be stuck in Products Liability long-term or just have to leave the firm. What if that happens? How long can I go without employment? Geez . . . why did I think this was a good idea?"

Because high achievers are competitive, they even compete with themselves (Chapter 4, "Predictors of Success," in the main book). And by creating additional anxiety by undermining their clarity and confidence, they could lose their voice. Even high achievers can be plagued by self-doubt. Modesty is attractive and even advised as associate lawyers advance in their firms and practice group areas. But "power bleeding," i.e. losing confidence with stammering and shuffling awkwardly in a courtroom or conference room as a response to a challenge, won't make you feel good about your performance in the moment and certainly won't inspire confidence in you from others. Healthy self-perspectives lead to healthy relationships and to brave, mature conversations, even if they aren't 100 percent comfortable. Excessively self-critical thoughts will deflate the most accomplished professional and quickly unravel courage and determination. Exercising the discipline of positive, internal non-judgmental thoughts will feed healthy, rational communication.

Monte needs to be calm, clear, and confident throughout the conversation.

Here's an exercise that could help you uncover internal critical thoughts that won't build confidence, and what to do about them. Fold a clean sheet of paper vertically down the middle and label the left column **Judgmental Thoughts** and the right column **Observing Thoughts**. This list should not be shared with anyone. In the left column, write anything negative you have ever thought about yourself or you remember being told about yourself. At the completion of this effort (and it may take a couple of pages) you may be in an introspective mood. Some will say they don't have judgmental thoughts and that's fine. In the main book, Chapter 9, "Owning Your Career," lays out a situation where an associate needs to tell some very bad news. The last things she needs are terrorizing thoughts that will only serve to increase her anxiety.

After the negative thoughts are written down, write a corollary, true statement under the Observing Thoughts column.

EXAMPLE

Judgmental Thoughts	Observing Thoughts
1. I should have known sooner what I wanted to do; I'm just so unfocused.	1. I'm relieved to be figuring out the direction of my practice.
2. I'll be awkward and uncomfortable as I tell Mark what I want to do. Somehow, I always disappoint people.	2. I am clear and confident in my decision and not wanting to disappoint Mark is normal.
3. I'm a wimp and will back down if pressured. Remember that time . . .	3. I am reasonable and considerate when pressured and not easily dissuaded.
4. Kent tried this at his firm and alienated himself permanently from his first boss. That's probably what'll happen.	4. Kent's experience is his; I will work to continue a professional relationship with Mark.
5. I don't deserve to be at this firm anyway.	5. I met the firm's standards for employment and my reviews have been positive and encouraging. They will be even more so when I change sections.

C. "Power Bleeding" vs. Powerful Communication

Also in the main book, Chapter 4, "Predictors of Success," we refer to "power bleeding" as the undesirable draining of confidence, evidenced by a change in your coloring, vocal tone or inflection, and verbal fluency. Some give a deer-caught-in-the-headlights look, others turn pale or red, and others stammer, shuffle, and lose eye contact. The following group exercise gives you the experience of observing someone as they try to convey confidence under stress. Be aware of how you feel when you know you're trying to bluff. You can do this with only one other person in your office or with another participant in a group training session where everyone is also pairing off. In either venue, face your partner.

a. Determine A and B status. The A's have come to report to their B partner that the $10,000 they owe them can't yet be paid back and they need an extension. This message will be delivered *silently and without gestures or facial expressions*. Looking into the eyes of the B's, the A's will feel what it's like to be powerless.

   Switch roles. The B's will now owe the money and again, *silently and without gestures or facial expressions*, they will feel their powerlessness.

b. Debrief the exercise:
   a. Each share what they sensed just by observing the muscle tone in the face and eyes and the overall energy of the powerless participant.
   b. Discuss the internal difference they felt when they were in the power position.
   c. Now add words, gestures, and facial expressions to the exercise, each taking the A and B roles. Debrief what each observes in themselves and of the other in both situations.

D. Building Rapport: Match and Mirror; Pace and Lead

Chapter 7 of the main book, "People Like to Do Business with People They Like" discusses the importance of being liked when working to establish trust and instill confidence in your abilities. The conversation with Mark will be more comfortable for both of them if Monte is in positive rapport with his mentor. This exercise will move persons in disagreement from alienation and frustration to connection and a re-stabilized relationship, even if they agree to disagree.

1. Again divide the group into pairs, with A and B status. Tell the A's to leave the room and go into the hall and that you'll join them in a minute. Be certain the door is closed while you tell the B's that they have 2 minutes to tell their A partner (simultaneously with the rest of the group) a brief story about their childhood, including:
   a. where they were born, and
   b. attended school . . .
   c. who was in the family . . .
   d. if they moved around . . .
   e. a memorable childhood lesson they've never forgotten (like getting caught telling a lie, or what it felt like to be targeted as a nerd, or learning that faking illness wasn't such a great idea, etc.)

2. While the B's are thinking about their story, rejoin the A's in the hall, tell them what the B's assignment is, then give the A's their assignment. Act uninterested for the first minute and then engage with them the second minute. Tell the A's not to overdo it, but suggest they check their watch or Blackberry, or fidget or frown. Tell them not to frustrate the B's too much, but encourage them to send the message they aren't fully engaged. Some will say they aren't good at role-playing, others might say their partner knows them well and will figure it out. Reinforce the idea that we don't want to anger the B's, only discourage them.

3. All A's return to the room and sit beside their B partner. Remind them to talk for 2 minutes and say, "Begin." At the 1 minute mark, turn or discard flipchart paper as if you were tidying up. At the 2 minute mark, call time and debrief. Ask:
   a. What was the experience of the B's when telling their story?
   b. Were they uninterested the entire time?
   c. If they became interested, what caused the change?

    d. Underreact to statements like, "I'm sure their assignment was to act bored."

4. Then reveal the assignment emphasizing that halfway through, the A's became interested because of the pre-arranged signal and agreement. You can expect that a B will say, "I thought they were bored at first because my life was uninteresting until I got to the college part. They perked up at that, so I went on some." Discuss:

    a. How it felt to be ignored . . .

    b. What did you try to increase interest?

    c. Who gave up and didn't care and thought now you remembered why you hate role-playing?

    d. Point out that giving attention satisfies many fundamental human needs (Chapter 2 of the main book, "What Lawyers Need"). *Connection* is established with good eye contact and facing them squarely. *Autonomy* is created by making them feel special with your attention, and *comfort* is satisfied through active listening (nodding and asking good questions).

5. Now have the B's leave the room and give the A's the same assignment: to share a life lesson learned while growing up. Rejoin the B's in the hall and give them the new assignment of interrupting often and asking overly detailed questions. Again emphasize not overdoing the assignment so to anger them; only frustrate them.

6. The B's then return to the room, sit with their former partner and begin this two minute exercise. At the two minute mark, call time and debrief. Ask:

    a. What was the A's experience, trying to tell their story?

    b. What did you do to keep the story progressing?

    c. Who gave up and just went with not being able to finish?

7. Reveal that the B's assignment was to interrupt and ask poor questions. Discuss the distinction between asking questions because you're intellectually curious (advised) and asking questions that take away control from the story-teller and frustrate the relationship. (Not advised.)

Applaud the A's who said they just went with it, and eventually got around to completing the story. This is matching and mirroring (Chapter 7 in the main book, "People Like to Do Business with People They Like") to create alignment and comfort toward the goal of building a relationship.

8. The final phase of this exercise is to ask the A's to return to the hall and instruct the B's to think of a trip story they can tell in two minutes. It can be a trip they have already taken or one coming up. Then join the A's in the hall.

9. Assign the A's the task of listening attentively and asking good questions with rare interruptions. But the main assignment is to physically mirror their B partner from the time they are seated. Warn them that you will say "freeze," not just "stop" at the end of this exercise.

10. As soon as they re-enter the room, they are to notice the posture and physical placement of their B partner in relationship to their chair and table. If B's are fidgeting with a pen, A's should fidget with a pen. If B's are facially expressive as they talk, A's follow them facially. Tell them not to scratch if they scratch; they'll be discovered. Subtlety is the key to creating comfort in the B's.

Observe the room, noticing the pairs physically matched and call the two minute stopping point by saying loudly, "freeze." Ask the B's if they could tell what the A assignment was. If you can tell someone figured it out during the role-playing, ask them last. You'll hear, "I think they were told to be good listeners." "They were told to do everything right this time." Rarely will you hear that they were told to mirror us, but you might.

Then reveal that the assignment was to mirror and ask everyone to look around. If the participants did freeze, they should still be in a mirrored relationship.

The lesson is that physical rapport (mirroring), when done subtly and for the purpose of creating comfort in another, can set up a bias for mental agreement. When people agree to disagree, it's often because there is comfort and rapport in the relationship that they may value.

Monte wants to mirror Mark physically and vocally. "Pace and lead" means to follow Mark's rate of speaking, his intensity, and overall tone. In the main book, Chapter 7, "People Like to Do Business with People They Like," we remind you that once you match someone physically, you can then change back to more natural behavior, more comfortable to you, and they probably will mirror you.

CHAPTER 4

Scenario # 2:
She Said; He Heard

The Monday morning docket call meant Greg would be receiving voice mail instruction for the day from the partner he worked with most often, Margarita. Driving to the courthouse, Margarita laid out her needs and priorities so Greg could get a running start. She wasn't ever sure how long the docket call would take but if he could cover some bases for her, the week would be manageable. Greg hated receiving instructions over the phone and had requested that she send an e-mail the night before or Monday morning before leaving home, but it didn't work for Margarita and her shareholder status trumped his mid level associate status, so she made it clear, he was to adapt to her style. Today's messages . . . cancel the client meeting for today (but was he to reschedule it also?), prepare deposition questions for Wednesday (but he'd need to read through the case file and that might mean the memo she'd asked him to prepare could be delayed), and follow up with Rudy regarding his view of Judge Simond's court (e-mail him, call him or go see him?) left him irritated, unclear, and uncertain. After some consideration, Greg decided that his first priority would be to work on the memo. When Margarita returned, she called Greg in to see how he'd progressed; upon learning he'd done nothing yet she threw up her arms and their conversation began . . .

Group Discussion Questions

1) What is Margarita's learning style? Visual, auditory, or kinesthetic? Greg's?
2) What are their personality style preferences? Intuitor, Thinker, Feeler, or Sensor?
3) Why didn't Greg do anything?
4) What response should he have to Margarita without blaming her for his inaction?
5) What's a good way for Greg to ask his clarifying questions?
6) Was Greg being obtuse, or overwhelmed or rebellious or none of these?

7) In the future, how might Greg get the information he needs over voice mail?

8) How should he execute "match and mirror" to avoid getting angry at Margarita?

Exercise: Learning Styles: Sensory Acuity

The main book's Chapter 5, "Biases, Baggage and Frames of Reference," discusses the challenge of trying to figure out what people mean beyond what they are saying. Margarita and Greg have had a classic miscommunication simply because they have very different learning styles. Additionally, Greg may need to learn how to request feedback and receive instruction for meeting Margarita's expectations. In the main book, Chapter 8 is concerned with the "Importance of Feedback." A 4-step process is outlined there that shows how to ask for feedback in a way that encourages a helpful response.

You may discover in the exercise that follows that you have a dominant learning style or a combination of styles.

SENSORY ACUITY

Discover your dominant learning style by answering the following questions. Score the exercise at the conclusion.

Agree = 10   Disagree = 5

1. ___ My friends know me as a good listener.
2. ___ I prefer movies with a relaxed pace and a plot that slowly unwinds over those that are full of action, noise and special effects.
3. ___ My idea of a great evening is when I can just stay home and wear comfortable clothing.
4. ___ I am inclined to make my first impression of people by the way they use their voice rather than by their looks or physical actions.
5. ___ I love to watch people go by at a shopping mall.
6. ___ I have a vivid imagination.
7. ___ I can hardly resist singing along with the radio whenever it's playing.
8. ___ I won't leave the house until I am certain that I look good.
9. ___ I can enjoy music only when it helps me to relax.
10. ___ I will go to certain movies just to see the "special effects," scenery or costumes.
11. ___ There is nothing that can relax me more than having my neck and shoulders rubbed.

12. ___ I spend a good deal of my leisure time on the telephone.
13. ___ I need to get up, stretch and move frequently.
14. ___ After a stressful day my body will feel tense; I frequently have a difficult time unwinding.
15. ___ I usually watch television or read while eating.
16. ___ I would rather listen to a storyteller than read a book.
17. ___ I have a clearly defined concept of what I want my life to be.
18. ___ I regularly listen to talk radio.
19. ___ I will usually judge people by their clothing and appearance more than by the way they speak or physically respond.
20. ___ I usually fidget or doodle while talking on the telephone.
21. ___ I will often spend time just listening to my tapes or CD's.
22. ___ I find it difficult to tune out noise and loud voices.
23. ___ I find it easy to hug someone whom I have just met.
24. ___ I will usually wait for my "gut feeling" to decide how I feel about a person.
25. ___ I am drawn to books with attractive, colorful covers.
26. ___ To me, there is nothing so stimulating as good conversation.
27. ___ I notice the décor and artwork when entering a room.
28. ___ I sing, hum or talk to myself while taking a shower.
29. ___ My office is color-coordinated and well decorated.
30. ___ For me there is nothing like a hot bath or shower to relieve stress and tension.

SENSORY ACUITY SCORING

Now use your response totals from above to figure out which mode of communication you prefer.

VISUAL Question Response Number	Total	AUDITORY Question Response Number	Total	KINESTHETIC Question Response Number	Total
5	___	1	___	2	___
6	___	4	___	3	___
8	___	7	___	9	___
10	___	12	___	11	___
15	___	16	___	13	___
17	___	18	___	14	___
19	___	21	___	20	___
25	___	22	___	23	___
27	___	26	___	24	___
29	___	28	___	30	___
TOTAL	___	**TOTAL**	___	**TOTAL**	___

Margarita seems to have a sensorial personality preference and an auditory learning style. She's doing many things at once, runs chronically late and never thinks that leaving verbal messages is anything but efficient. Greg appears to be a thinker and have a more visual orientation to receiving information. He needs to write down everything he hears via voice mail and this could be time consuming. He'll need to go over and over the message for every word and work at interpreting her tone for her intentions. Reading it back will give him the visual stimulation he needs to be able to move on his assignments. He'll need e-mails as often as possible or to take notes when he's with Margarita. Visually oriented people can become confused by the content unless graphics, schematics or icons/photos accompany the dialogue. He can also request that Margarita give the message in segments or divide the assignments into a priorities list. This requires desire and discipline on Margarita's part so he'll need to make a proper request, as laid out in Chapter 8 of the main book, and he'll need to start with "I need your help."

CHAPTER 5

Scenario # 3:
Reduced Hours, Please

Allison is the proud mom of two beautiful children, Kenedy (4 years) and Benjamin (9 months). After having Ben, she thought she would be able to juggle her career, her kids and her community obligations just as before—it would be hard but she would do it. But 9 months after Ben was born, she'd hit her breaking point. She has decided that she has to go to Ramon, her supervising attorney, to tell him she needs to do something about her work situation because it is not working for her and her family. She would prefer to work out a reduced hour arrangement, but she is willing to quit altogether, if that is her only option. She plans to tell him that, although she has appreciated his and the firm's patience and understanding when she had to leave early or miss work altogether because one of her kids had been sick, her current arrangement is not giving her the balance she wants and needs in her life. And, although she is actually at a point in her career where she is happier practicing law than she ever has been, her family life is suffering. If something must be sacrificed it is going to be her career and not her kids. She isn't nervous that Ramon would erupt with anger—though he would undoubtedly be disappointed—but rather, she is afraid that a reduced hour arrangement would not be acceptable to the firm. And she doesn't really want to have to quit a job she loves. She is concerned that the practice of law is still somewhat of a man's world and this particular trail had not been blazed by another woman at her firm. Though very nervous, Allison makes a lunch appointment with Ramon for the following day.

Group Discussion Questions

1) What's the best preparation Allison can have for this meeting? Should she preview the subject of the conversation in an e-mail to Ramon or just surprise him at lunch?

2) If Allison is a "Thinker" and Ramon is a "Feeler," what should she anticipate about Ramon's reaction? (*Clue: "Thinkers" tend to be more analytical and base their arguments on*

facts; "feelers" tend to rely on stories and examples for persuasion, and take situations personally.)

3) How much small talk should transpire before Allison gets to the point?

4) Will it help Allison's request to bring testimonials from other senior attorneys in other firms speaking to the success of part-time lawyers in their firms? *(Clue: When persuading a "feeler," hearing words from other persons can help, especially if they offer to speak on the phone or face-to-face of the success.)*

1) If Ramon takes her wanting to go to part-time personally, he might think she hasn't liked working for him and that he hasn't been supportive. What can Allison do to calm his affront short of patronizing him?

Exercises

Chapter 5, "Biases, Baggage, and Frames of Reference," in the main book discusses personality styles and the importance of anticipating the styles of others when presenting your point of view.

A. Personality Style Survey

Solid self-awareness, an important element for emotional intelligence, suggests that the better you understand yourself in a variety of settings and interactions with a number of elements, i.e. time pressures; cultural assumptions; interruptions, the better you will manage goals, conversations, stress and people. This brief assessment will determine your preference for interacting in the world. The objective is to understand that people may think and behave differently from you but that doesn't mean they are wrong. An additional objective is to learn language for "reading" people to help develop rapport with them.

INSTRUCTIONS FOR TAKING THE INSTRUMENT

It is not possible to get right or wrong answers on this questionnaire. This is a survey that helps you understand your approach to people and situations.

You will read 11 self-descriptive statements, each of which is followed by 4 possible endings, marked a., b., c., and d. In the box, you are to indicate the order in which you feel EACH ending is most like you. Put the number 6 for the ending most like you, 4 for the next most like you, 2 for the next most like you, and 0 for the least like you. Each numerically marked row of boxes must have a 6, 4, 2, and 0 in some order. NO TIES. This is a forced choice inventory, so even if none of them seem like you, you must put a ranking in the box anyway.

Fill in the boxes; then total the columns. The sum should be 144—that's to double check that you haven't forgotten how to add without a calculator.

Remember to work swiftly; your first response is probably the most accurately reflective of your preferences.

PERSONALITY STYLE PREFERENCES

1. You supervise a task group whose morale has deteriorated rapidly in recent weeks. Your course of action will be to:
   a. Suggest that each group member answer a series of questions in order to compile data and pinpoint specific problem areas.
   b. Meet with the group and brainstorm ideas for a new project in order to reduce the pressure of current concerns.
   c. Ignore the strategic issues and impress upon the group the critical nature of upcoming deadlines.
   d. Talk with each person in the group. Get a feel for his/her problems. Be sympathetic and understanding.

2. You have the responsibility for presenting a new project to your superiors. In planning your presentation, you would be most likely to:
   a. Make detailed outlines, in writing, and supply figures and other data to supplement your presentation.
   b. Convey your excitement about the innovative ideas and long-range impact of your project.
   c. Impress them with the positive short-term results you anticipate and the urgency of implementing your recommendations.
   d. Stress the importance of your project to the morale of your task group.

3. When you have a conflict with a firm lawyer, you will most often:
   a. Remain cool; ask the other person to meet with you; plan carefully the key points you want to enumerate.
   b. Occupy yourself with other things in order to relieve the tension.

Alternative Actions			
A	B	C	D

(rows labeled 1, 2, 3, 4, 5, 6, 7, 8, 9, 10, 11, Total)

    c. Jump right in and attempt to convince the other person of the positive aspects of your point of view.

    d. Encourage the other person to express feelings and try to understand his/her position even if you don't agree.

4. Your ideal working environment is one in which you are allowed to:
   a. Handle detailed or complicated projects efficiently.
   b. Come up with create new ideas.
   c. Make decisions and see immediate results.
   d. Interact freely with other lawyers.

5. Your superiors probably see you as:
   a. A persevering and dependable person.
   b. A person of vision with considerable leadership skills and self confidence.
   c. A person who accepts challenges and gets results.
   d. An outgoing person who gets along well with everyone.

6. In a crisis situation, your first action is most likely to be:
   a. Develop a logical plan for solving the problem.
   b. Withdraw until the storm passes.
   c. Act quickly. If it doesn't work out, you can always change it later.
   d. Emotional—you feel angry or frustrated.

7. When a peer criticizes or comments on your work, do you:
   a. Ask the other person to enumerate specifics.
   b. Ignore the person and continue with your original idea.
   c. Argue and defend your point of view.
   d. Wonder if he/she dislikes you; you suspect ulterior motives.

8. You have been in your current position for some time and feel you are qualified for a promotion. In influencing the decision maker, you'll be most likely to:
   a. Write a memo outlining your past accomplishments, current activities, and potential contributions.
   b. Share your long-term personal goals and show how they relate to the firm's objectives.
   c. Show how you can help both you and the firm grow in a strategically agreed on direction.
   d. Stress your loyalty and positive personal feelings about the organization.

9. You probably find it difficult to:
   a. Show sympathy and understanding of people's personal problems.
   b. Follow through on projects you've initiated.
   c. Be enthusiastic about long-range organizational goals.
   d. Give negative feedback to subordinates or colleagues.

10. In managing your time, you usually prefer to:
    a. Plan each day's activities and set priorities.
    b. Spend time with long-range visioning and strategic direction.
    c. Create action plans for achieving goals.
    d. Work on the most interesting projects first; procrastinate on routine things.

11. Your overall personal goal is to:
    a. Work hard and invest intelligently so you can enjoy a comfortable retirement.
    b. Contribute to significant new trends in the legal world.
    c. Be recognized by others as a successful lawyer.
    d. Enjoy life and bring joy to people you care about.

UNDERSTANDING YOUR SCORE

Once completed, circle the highest score or scores, if there are ties. Then put a box around other scores within 6 points of the high score. The circled score(s) is your strongest personality preference and the boxed score(s) is your back-up style(s).

"72 is the highest score you could get if you answer "6" every time in one category. "0" is the lowest score you could get if you answer "0" every time in that category. The greater or lower the score suggests the intensity of your preference for one style over another.

"A" = "T," Thinker

"B" = "I," Intuitor (sometimes referred to as "N" style)

"C" = "S," Sensor

"D" = "F," Feeler

4 COMMUNICATION STYLES

	(B) INTUITOR (Ideas)	**(A)** THINKER (Facts)	**(D)** FEELER (Feelings)	**(C)** SENSOR (Action)
Function	conceptual; thinks in images; long-range vision	analytical; thinks in columns; careful; wary	feeling; valuing; thinks with emotional system; understands through emotional reactions	action-oriented; thinks of implementation; understands through the senses (seeing, hearing, touching, tasting)
Key words	the "big picture"; ideas; strategic; innovative; unique; possibilities	logical; stable; rational; facts; research; data; orderly	values; spontaneous; persuasive; self-reflective; feelings; gut reactions	action; momentum; doer; shoots from the hip; bottom line results
Positives	original; creative; full of new methods; visionary; problem-solver; rearranges old pieces into new patterns; sees long-term effect; exciting	consistent producer; thoughtful; cool under pressure; calm; stabilizing; objective	draws out feelings of others; skilled in communication; builder of team work; nurturer of individuals/groups; can read between the lines	translates ideas into action; moves mountains; attention to detail; driving force in group or organization; moves ahead with determination
Challenges	unrealistic; in an ivory tower; idea is wonderful but won't work; need for so much planning time	lacks enthusiasm; plays it too safe; rigid; likely to say "no" first if pressured for a quick decision	over-reactive; relies on gut feeling—not facts; too concerned with people's sensitivities; impulsive; overly sentimental; guilt-ridden; defensive	fails to consider long range consequences; high speed leaves little room for others who march to a different drummer
Rhythm	Glide and zoom	steady march	changes from waltz to bunny hop	dead run followed by a collapse

HOW TO BUILD RAPPORT WITH OTHER STYLES

	(B) INTUITOR (Ideas)	(A) THINKER (Facts)	(D) FEELER (Feelings)	(C) SENSOR (Action)
To influence them:	1. Relate to the "big picture"	1. Be researched (facts, data, options)	1. Be warm and personal	1. Be brief
	2. Talk in terms of the future	2. Be very businesslike, specific and detailed	2. Be enthusiastic	2. Get right to the point
	3. Show interest in his/her creative concepts	3. Be low-key, conservative and cautious	3. Stress long-term personal relationships	3. Use simple, practical examples
	4. Show where your idea or project fits in the grand design	4. Emphasize soundness, reliability, and statistics	4. Support your service, idea or solution with first-hand testimonials and personalized feedback	4. Indicate urgency
	5. Give him/her time; plan an unhurried meeting	5. Ask for data-oriented feedback	5. Be helpful and supportive	5. Emphasize results
	6. Be imaginative in your approach	6. Talk slowly and clearly	6. Smile, use eye contact	6. Be on time
Their listening stance	Listens for innovation and a new approach; doesn't hear "it can't be done"; mind jumps, fears the ordinary; wants to play with ideas	Listens in terms of categories; deals with syntactic and semantic rather than pragmatic; denies feelings; values rational appraisal	Listens almost entirely with feelings and too little with head; has a fear of hearing alarming messages; avoids conflict; focuses on presence or absence of emotional connection	Not interested in whys and wherefores; wants direct answers to questions; insists on all/none, right/wrong, black/white

B. Emptying

In the main book, Chapter 9, "Owning Your Career," discusses the importance of keeping your cool, especially with difficult conversations, fierce personalities and surprising urgencies. If a lot is going on in your life, you're juggling stress both personally and professionally, we say you could be too "full" to risk that some of the unacknowledged emotion due to stress could come out in unprofessional ways that would embarrass you and cause great discomfort to those you're around.

Allison may have a lot on her mind as she joins Ramon for lunch. Right before coming, she may have heard disturbing news about her neighbor's on-going health struggles; she might be tired from caring for a sick child in the night; she might have just looked at the holiday bills; she may be worried she can't get in all her needed CLE credits by the deadline. Whatever is on her mind, she needs to empty it out to be able to focus. If she goes in "full," she could over-react to a comment from Ramon; get more intense and urgent about her decision than she planned on; or tear up.

Each participant is to write out a list of thoughts that have crossed their mind today, OR

Select a partner to share these thoughts, to get them out of the way. The partner only listens with no comment or affective response.

C.　Rehearse the Conversation

Allison needs to know with as much clarity and conviction she can muster what her specific request is. Does she want to quit? Does she want reduced hours? How much reduced? Clarity is powerful. Will she walk away from the job if the request isn't granted? By when must she make the change? "Reduced hours" isn't an amount and "soon" isn't a time. To help her clarity and perhaps confront the reality of the request, she should role-play the conversation with a friend or colleague who's willing to play Ramon and be tough. If she can anticipate the possible irrational or emotional response to this important and potentially uncomfortable conversation, she'll be proud of her conduct and increase her chances of Ramon being supportive. Chapter 6, "Dialogue, Not Monologue, Creates Relationships," in the main book is a good point of reference.

For this exercise, select "A" and "B" partners; someone you haven't worked with before. Each selects a real conversation that he/she wants to rehearse. Select one that's not too personal but one you could use some help with.

On a blank sheet each participant writes:

1. What's the content issue? *(Allison's would be: I want more time with my kids.)*
2. What's the desired change or request? *(Allison's might be: I want to work three quarter's time; leave at 3:00 daily; OR leave at noon Thursday and not come in at all on Friday; OR . . . .)*

3. How you feel about the issue.
4. How you are anticipating the other party will feel about it. *(Consider personality styles here.)*
5. How do I complicate the issue and take responsibility for it.
6. What's your commitment to resolve the situation in the best interest of all parties?

Decide who goes first and briefly explain the relationship you have with this individual you need to speak with and what complications there may be in terms of a power imbalance, or personal history with them or anything pertinent that might create discomfort.

Also, ask your partner what personality style they are, tell them your style and adjust your approach accordingly.

When each has finished the rehearsal of a desired conversation, ask for two volunteers to role-play Allison and Ramon in Scenario #3. Ramon's possible "Feeler" response will be emotionally based: facial and vocal expression of disappointment; defensiveness; and perhaps too much interest in creating fear in Allison—fear of less money, loss of reputation, not able to return at a later date and achieve partner or shareholder status.

Allison will attempt a rational, logical approach, both in content and vocal tone. She will emphasize her measured analysis, having weighed all alternatives. She probably won't admit to any emotional pain around her request.

Ramon will assert that she's an excellent technical lawyer but he'll worry that her request will reflect negatively on his supervisory abilities.

Debrief this role-play with the entire group. Suggest ways these two opposite styles can build rapport and eventually agree to disagree with her decision and remain respected colleagues.

CHAPTER 6

Scenario # 4:
The Small-Talk Challenge

Anupama, a 6th-year associate, was delighted and somewhat nervous that a senior partner, Spencer Marks in her practice group, had invited her to lunch to meet one of the firm's premier clients. Jaston Coleman, Chair of a major telecommunications company in Canada, and his wife were in town briefly to attend a family wedding. Spencer hoped by introducing Anupama, Jaston would learn more about the business opportunities in India, an emerging telecommunications market. Anupama arrived ahead of Spencer at the Four Seasons dining room and was escorted to the table where Mr. Coleman was seated. She'd hoped to be introduced by Spencer, but he was running late and she'd just have to face her social shyness head-on if she was to develop business relationships. As Mr. Coleman rose from his chair to greet her, he tipped it backward to the floor and spilled wine down the leg of his suit. Anupama blushed from the embarrassment of the situation and his discomfort and said . . .

Group Discussion Questions

1) What are the inherent potential discomforts experienced by Anupama as well as Jaston Coleman?
2) Should she have waited at the hostess desk for Spencer, even knowing he was running a little late?
3) Should Anupama seat herself as the waiter sees to Mr. Coleman's chair and wet trouser leg?
4) How should Anupama enter into this business conversation after observing the awkward accident?
5) When Mr. Coleman comments that she's awfully attractive and young to know about international business deals, how should she respond?

Chapter 6, "Dialogue, Not Monologue, Creates Relationships," in the main book discusses aspects of small talk and conversation.

Anupama intended to rely on the senior partner to create comfort for her, especially initially, at this lunch. He was to introduce her glowingly and position her as a trusted member of Coleman's legal team. But now she faces a need to think on her feet, get comfortable the best she can, and relate to Mr. Coleman professionally.

6) How can she communicate empathy for his plight without diminishing his seniority and esteemed status?
7) As decorum is re-established and they begin to converse, what is her role?
8) When Spencer finally arrives, does she initiate the story of the spilled wine?
9) How much of her personal life (coming to America for her advanced degrees; leaving her family behind in India) should she share with Coleman?
10) Wanting to show interest in Mr. Coleman and his personal reason for being in town, does she initiate questions about his family life?

Exercise

Starting and Maintaining a Conversation

Even in the face of shyness, conversational ease is important to developing professional relationships. Chapter 6, "Dialogue, Not Monologue Creates Relationships" declares that conversations change perceptions, awareness, and understandings. Executed gracefully, conversations can positively boost careers.

Create pairs by choosing the person you know least in the group and have them select A or B status. Ask that they spread out over the room to give them as much privacy as possible and to diminish distractions. Ask the A partner to begin a conversation that must last 10 minutes, with no particular goal in mind. When time is called, debrief the exercise by discussing the following questions and capturing them on the flipchart.

1. What were the most challenging aspects of this exercise from both the A and B perspective?
2. Who talked most and why?
3. What surprises were learned?

4. How many stories were told?
5. How soon did you stop wanting the exercise to be over?
6. What approaches worked? What didn't work?
7. Was there comfort with silence and pausing?
8. How did you gage sincerity, ease and likeability of the other?

Now ask the B partner to begin a conversation with the goal of persuading the A to either:

1. Vote for your candidate, or
2. Change practice group focus, or
3. Volunteer to help in a fundraiser for a charity of your choice, or
4. Increase their exercise habits and decrease sugar/fat consumption, or
5. Consider buying the same model car you drive.

The conversation must last 10 minutes; then the debrief commences. Ask:

1. What were all the ways this conversation was different from the first?
2. When were each comfortable, or not?
3. How was tension created or avoided?
4. If disagreement prevailed, how did it affect the relationship?

CHAPTER 7

Scenario # 5:
Undervalued on the Eve of Trial

Frank practices in the medical malpractice group at Harris and Gilkerson, P.C. He likes defending doctors but, to him, there is nothing worse than doing comprehensive status reports to the malpractice carrier—especially on a case he has just inherited from Eduardo, another lawyer at the firm. But it has been about six months since the last report has been sent and the trial is two weeks away. It is time for an update. After several hours of reading through the file, Frank determines what he believes to be the range of potential exposure for Dr. Scott, whom he now represents—and it is significant. There is a bid problem. Frank's assessment of potential exposure far exceeds the assessment the original (and less experienced) attorney had communicated to the carrier in the previous report. Frank is worried that the doctor could be exposed to additional damages totaling $2 million more than had been previously estimated. How in the world is he going to break this to Dr. Scott without making Eduardo look completely incompetent, or worse yet, exposing the firm to a potential malpractice claim?

Group Discussion Questions

1) What are Frank's alternatives?
2) How should he begin when speaking with the client? (*Clue: The best way to tell bad news is quickly.*)
3) What medium should he use, ie. e-mail, face-to-face, or voice mail, with Eduardo? His supervising lawyer?
4) If Dr. Scott becomes furious and angry at the original lawyer, what does Frank say?
5) How much should Frank apologize? (*Clue: When people apologize for anything . . . being late; causing stress; mis-reading the e-mail . . . the other side can feel momentarily powerful. Two or three times should be plenty.*)
6) What interpersonal communication skills should he exercise? (*Clue: Eye contact; fluent, strong voice; arms un-crossed*)

7) Other than tell bad news, what are Frank's goals for the interactions?

Exercises

Yield, Align and Move to Action

Chapter 9, "Owning Your Career," suggests that moving quickly
and directly to take responsibility for errors, without losing long-
term credibility, will move the conversation to possible solutions.

As much as Frank needs to quickly report the mistake, he first needs
to discuss the situation with Eduardo to get background information and seek advice from a senior lawyer's perspective.

Recommended steps:
1) Prepare your strategy and verbally role-play with a colleague.
2) State the situation factually; what happened.
3) Allow the reaction from the other person.
4) Move into alignment with them; agree their perspective is a
fair one.
5) Mirror them physically, rather than just stand or sit passively
or stoically. (*That can anger some because they don't get it that you
get it.*)
6) Move to possible solutions.

As a group exercise, ask for two volunteers to role-play. Read
Scenario #5 aloud before beginning.

Take 1:

Frank should be stoic, have a dozen excuses, blame the other attorney and tell the client she's over-reacting.

Dr. Scott should become very upset and accuse Frank's firm and
the previous attorney of unprofessional behavior and ineptitude.
Voices should be raised and nothing resolved.

Before Take 2 of the role-play, have the 2 stand and face each other,
put their hands up chest high and firmly press against the other
pair of hands. To exert effort, each may need to put one foot back
so to really lean into the hands of the other. As they press, each trying to exert more force than the other, suggest to the group that
this is the result you get (tension, effort, no resolution) unless someone yields. (*This is a martial arts concept and is referred to in Getting To*

Yes, the Harvard Negotiation Project, by Roger Fisher and William Ury, Penguin Books, 1981, in the chapter on Jujitsu Negotiations.)

When Frank puts his hands down and stops pushing, he doesn't lose; in fact, Dr. Scott's footing will be lost momentarily and Frank can then step to the doctor's side, aligned, and he becomes equally involved in the next step, resolution.

Take 2

Frank should now follow the recommended steps outlined previously.

1) Again, prepare your strategy and verbally role-play with a colleague.
2) State the situation factually; what happened.
3) Allow the reaction from the other person.
4) Move into alignment with them; agree that their perspective is a fair one.
5) Mirror them physically, rather than just stand or sit passively or stoically.
6) Move to possible solutions.

The client doesn't have to be happy. But see what happens, even if it's just a role-play, when yielding and aligning are used to get you quickly to resolution.

Debrief the difference between Take 1 and Take 2.

B. Feel, Felt, Found

In Chapter 9 in the main book, "Owning Your Career," we discuss how to deal with a big mistake. "Feel, Felt, Found" is a good approach to a tough conversation. It is a technique for overcoming strong feelings resulting from mistakes made in the face of every good intention. The goal is to quickly acknowledge and then move through strong feelings toward rational action.

Divide the group into pairs who then determine A and B status. Ask the A's to be Frank and come up with various approaches to using the FEEL, FELT, FOUND technique. Example:

FEEL: "I see how angry and disappointed you are right now." (name the feeling)

FELT: "I would feel the same in your shoes and I'm certainly disappointed and frustrated with the situation." (identify with them)

FOUND: "With your agreement, we will move ahead with our case knowing there is an increased exposure and consult with you every step of the way." Or "We suggest that an appropriate settlement offer would be in the neighborhood of $_____. We have discussed this with the insurance carriers and they are in agreement." (suggest a solution)

Let the B's evaluate the approach and make suggestions.

This won't create instant happiness; it will affirm the client's feelings and responses and move the conversation to the action steps rather than letting it bog down in negative emotions, accusations and defensiveness. Frank may need to repeat the "feel, felt, found" formula a couple of times before the conversation shifts

CONCLUSION

Even with all the expertise offered in the book and manual, good communication is more art than science and improvement is an ongoing process. Not every approach you try will work, but every experience you have trying will teach you something. There are no off-the-shelf formulas. Every stage of your career will require different awareness, understanding, and behavior as you move through the law firm hierarchy. Our hope is that we've added to your insight, skills and advancement as you become more competent, confident and compelled to achieve your professional goals.

INDEX

The Legal Career Guide:
From Law Student to Lawyer,
Fifth Edition

By Gary A. Munneke and Ellen Wayne

This is a step-by-step guide for planning a law career, preparing and executing a job search, and moving into the market. Whether you're considering a solo career, examining government or corporate work, joining a medium or large firm, or focusing on an academic career, this book is filled with practical advice that will help you find your personal niche in the legal profession. This book will also help you make the right choices in building resumes, making informed career decisions, and taking the first step toward career success.

Women-at-Law: Lessons Learned Along the Pathways to Success

By Phyllis Horn Epstein

Discover how women lawyers in a wide variety of practice settings are meeting the challenges of competing in an often all-consuming profession without sacrificing their desire for a multidimensional life. Women-at-Law provides a wealth of practical guidance and direction from experienced women lawyers who share their life stories and advice to inspire and encourage others by offering solutions to the challenges—personal and professional. You'll learn that, with some effort, a motivated woman can redirect her career, her home life, and her interests, in the long journey that is a successful life. If you are a law student, a practicing lawyer, or simply a woman considering a career

The Lawyer's Guide to Balancing Life and Work, Second Edition

By George W. Kaufman

This newly updated and revised Second Edition is written specifically to help lawyers achieve professional and personal satisfaction in their career. Writing with warmth and seasoned wisdom, George Kaufman examines how the profession has changed over the last five year, then offers philosophical approaches, practical examples, and valuable exercises to help lawyers reconcile their goals and expectations with the realities and demands of the legal profession. Interactive exercises are provided throughout the text and on the accompanying CD, to help you discover how to reclaim your life. New lawyers, seasoned veterans, and those who have personal relationships to lawyers will all benefit from this insightful book.

How to Build and Manage a
Personal Injury Practice, Second Edition

By K. William Gibson

Written exclusively for personal injury practitioners, this indispensable resource explores everything from choosing the right office space to measuring results of your marketing campaign. Author Bill Gibson has carefully constructed this "how-to" manual—highlighting all the tactics, technology, and practical tools necessary for a profitable practice, including how to write a sound business plan, develop an accurate financial forecast, maximize your staff while minimizing costs, and more.

How to Build and Manage an
Entertainment Law Practice

By Gary Greenberg

This book addresses a variety of issues critical to establishing a successful entertainment law practice including getting started, preparing a business plan, getting your foot in the door, creating the right image, and marketing your entertainment law practice. The book discusses the basic differences between entertainment law and other types of law practice and provides guidance for avoiding common pitfalls. In addition, an extensive appendix contains sample agreements, forms, letters, and checklists common to entertainment law practitioners. Includes a diskette containing the essential appendix templates, forms and checklists for easy implementation!

How to Build and Manage an Estates Practice,
Second Edition

By Daniel B. Evans

Whether you aim to define your "niche" in estates law, or market your estates practice on the Internet, this valuable guide can help you make a practice a success. Chapters are logically organized to lead you through the essential stages of developing your specialty practice and include practical, proven advice for everything from organizing estate planning and trust administration files . . . to conducting estate planning interviews . . . to implementing alternative billing strategies . . . to managing your workload (and staff!). Appendices include such sample documents as: an estate planning fee agreement, an estate administration fee agreement, an estate administration schedule, will execution instructions, and more.

The Successful Lawyer: Powerful Strategies for Transforming Your Practice
By Gerald A. Riskin
Available as a Book, Audio-CD Set, or Combination Package!
Global management consultant and trusted advisor to many of the world's largest law firms, Gerry Riskin goes beyond simple concept or theory and delivers a book packed with practical advice that you can implement right away. By using the principles found in this book, you can live out your dreams, embrace success, and awaken your firm to its full potential. Large law firm or small, managing partners and associates in every area of practice—all can benefit from the information contained in this book. With this book, you can attract what you need and desire into your life, get more satisfaction from your practice and your clients, and do so in a systematic, achievable way.

How to Start and Build a Law Practice, Platinum Fifth Edition
By Jay G Foonberg
This classic ABA bestseller has been used by tens of thousands of lawyers as the comprehensive guide to planning, launching, and growing a successful practice. It's packed with over 600 pages of guidance on identifying the right location, finding clients, setting fees, managing your office, maintaining an ethical and responsible practice, maximizing available resources, upholding your standards, and much more. You'll find the information you need to successfully launch your practice, run it at maximum efficiency, and avoid potential pitfalls along the way. If you're committed to starting—and growing—your own practice, this one book will give you the expert advice you need to make it succeed for years to come.

The Lawyer's Field Guide to Effective Business Development
By William J. Flannery, Jr.
This book is much more than a "survival guide"—it is a "success guide." Having trained more than 10,000 lawyers from around the world in client relationship management, business development and effective communication skills, William J. Flannery, an ex-IBM executive and J.D., focuses on practical ideas and approaches for business growth and relationship improvement. Flannery's approach to winning and retaining long-term, attractive clients is detailed and sensible. He proves that with the right approaches, the appropriate homework and diligence, and a little bit of courage, any lawyer can not only be smart, but effective as a client relationship manager and advocate.

The Law Firm Associate's Guide to Personal Marketing and Selling Skills
By Catherine Alman MacDonagh and Beth Marie Cuzzone
This is the first volume in ABA's new groundbreaking Law Firm Associates Development Series, created to teach important skills that associates and other lawyers need to succeed at their firms, but that they may have not learned in law school. This volume focuses on personal marketing and sales skills. It covers creating a personal marketing plan, finding people within your target market, preparing for client meetings, "asking" for business, realizing marketing opportunities, keeping your clients, staying in touch with your network inside and outside the firm, and more. An accompanying trainer's manual illustrating how to best structure the sessions and use the book is available to firms to facilitate group training sessions.

Many law firms expect their new associates to hit the ground running when they are hired on. Although firms often take the time to bring these associates up to speed on client matters, they can be reluctant to invest the time needed to train them how to improve personal skills such as marketing. This book will serve as a brief, easy-to-digest primer for associates on how to develop and use marketing and selling techniques.

The Lawyer's Guide to Marketing Your Practice, Second Edition
Edited by James A. Durham and Deborah McMurray
This book is packed with practical ideas, innovative strategies, useful checklists, and sample marketing and action plans to help you implement a successful, multi-faceted, and profit-enhancing marketing plan for your firm. Organized into four sections, this illuminating resource covers: Developing Your Approach; Enhancing Your Image; Implementing Marketing Strategies and Maintaining Your Program. Appendix materials include an instructive primer on market research to inform you on research methodologies that support the marketing of legal services. The accompanying CD-ROM contains a wealth of checklists, plans, and other sample reports, questionnaires, and templates—all designed to make implementing your marketing strategy as easy as possible!

The Busy Lawyer's Guide to Success: Essential Tips to Power Your Practice
By Reid F. Trautz and Dan Pinnington
Busy lawyers do not have dozens of extra hours to conduct research looking for new tips and ideas to streamline and enhance their practice of law. They need "just-in-time" learning to acquire the knowledge necessary to build their practices. This convenient pocket guide is the "best ever" collection of practical tips, ideas, and techniques to help you survive, thrive, and find success in the practice of law.

30-Day Risk-Free Order Form
Call Today! 1-800-285-2221
Monday–Friday, 7:30 AM – 5:30 PM, Central Time

Qty	Title	LPM Price	Regular Price	Total
_____	The Legal Career Guide: From Law Student to Lawyer, Fifth Edition (5110479)	$ 29.95	$ 34.95	$_____
_____	Women-at-Law: Lessons Learned Along the Pathways to Success (5110509)	39.95	49.95	$_____
_____	The Lawyer's Guide to Balancing Life and Work, Second Edition (5110566)	29.95	39.95	$_____
_____	How to Build and Manage a Personal Injury Practice, Second Edition (5110575)	54.95	64.95	$_____
_____	How to Build and Manage an Entertainment Law Practice (5110453)	54.95	64.95	$_____
_____	How to Build and Manage an Estates Practice, Second Edition (5110421)	44.95	54.95	$_____
_____	The Successful Lawyer—Book Only (5110531)	64.95	84.95	$_____
_____	The Successful Lawyer—Audio CDs Only (5110532)	129.95	149.95	$_____
_____	The Successful Lawyer—Audio CDs/Book Combination (5110533)	174.95	209.95	$_____
_____	How to Start and Build a Law Practice, Platinum Fifth Edition (5110508)	57.95	69.95	$_____
_____	The Lawyer's Field Guide to Effective Business Development (5110578)	49.95	59.95	$_____
_____	The Law Firm Associate's Guide to Personal Marketing and Selling Skills (5110582)	39.95	49.95	$_____
_____	The Lawyer's Guide to Marketing Your Practice, Second Edition (5110500)	79.95	89.95	$_____
_____	The Busy Lawyer's Guide to Success: Essential Tips to Power Your Practice (5110687)	44.95	69.95	$_____

*Postage and Handling	
$10.00 to $24.99	$5.95
$25.00 to $49.99	$9.95
$50.00 to $99.99	$12.95
$100.00 to $349.99	$17.95
$350 to $499.99	$24.95

**Tax
DC residents add 5.75%
IL residents add 10.25%

*Postage and Handling	$_____
**Tax	$_____
TOTAL	$_____

PAYMENT

❑ Check enclosed (to the ABA)

❑ Visa   ❑ MasterCard   ❑ American Express

_____

Account Number   Exp. Date   Signature

Name _____ Firm _____

Address _____

City _____ State _____ Zip _____

Phone Number _____ E-Mail Address _____

Guarantee

If—for any reason—you are not satisfied with your purchase, you may return it within 30 days of receipt for a complete refund of the price of the book(s). No questions asked!

Mail: ABA Publication Orders, P.O. Box 10892, Chicago, Illinois 60610-0892
♦ Phone: 1-800-285-2221 ♦ FAX: 312-988-5568

E-Mail: abasvcctr@abanet.org ♦ Internet: http://www.lawpractice.org/catalog